Joke & Riddle
BONANZA

MICHAEL J. PELLOWSKI

STERLING CHILDREN'S BOOKS
New York

STERLING CHILDREN'S BOOKS
New York

An Imprint of Sterling Publishing Co., Inc.
1166 Avenue of the Americas
New York, NY 10036

ISBN 978-1-4549-2247-6

Distributed in Canada by Sterling Publishing Co., Inc.
c/o Canadian Manda Group, 664 Annette Street
Toronto, Ontario, Canada M6S 2C8
Distributed in the United Kingdom by GMC Distribution Services
Castle Place, 166 High Street, Lewes, East Sussex, England BN7 1XU
Distributed in Australia by NewSouth Books
45 Beach Street, Coogee, NSW 2034, Australia

For information about custom editions, special sales, and premium and
corporate purchases, please contact Sterling Special Sales at 800-805-5489
or specialsales@sterlingpublishing.com.

Manufactured in Canada

Lot #:
2 4 6 8 10 9 7 5 3 1
07/17

sterlingpublishing.com

Design by Ryan Thomann

Contents

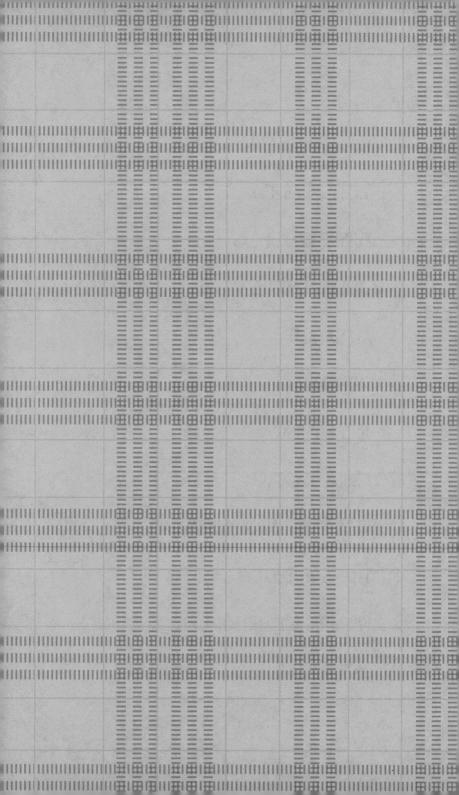

1

FRIGHTFULLY FUNNY

What giant buzzing insects lived long ago?

Beehistoric monsters.

What does a Brontosaurus have on the end
of its feet?

Brontoes!

Which dinosaur is a body builder?

Tyrannosaurus Flex.

What monster lives in the mountains and
alters men's suits?

The Abominable Sewman.

When does a monster duck wake up?

At the quack of doom.

What do female monsters discuss when they're alone together?

Ghoul talk.

What's noisy and performs at parades in space?

A Martian band.

What peculiar guy is in charge of the Starship Enterprise?

Captain Quirk.

——SILLY SPACE BOOKS——

How to Build Robots by Ann Droid

Successful Rocket Launches by Count M. Down

Heavenly Bodies by Lotta Stars

Space Weapons by Ray Gunn

What is wooly and from outer space?

A Ewe-F-O.

CARVED ON
THE TOMBSTONE
OF R2-D2:

"Rust in Peace"

HA HA HA HA HA HA HA HA HA HA HA

What do you call a cartoon character from the moon?

A lunar tune.

What do you get if you cross a yellow mummy and a green mummy?

A golden mouldy.

NUTTY NOTICE

The mummy's watch is an old-timer.

Which ghost came from the planet Krypton?

Spookerman.

What do trendy ghosts wear?

Designer boo jeans.

Which monster makes designer jeans?

Calvin Frankenklein.

Where does Calvin Frankenklein live?

In Pantsylvania.

Where do monster TV shows go when they're taken off the air?

To Cancelvania.

What did the girl say to her invisible boyfriend?

"I can't see you anymore."

What monster lives in a clothes dryer?

Kling Kong.

What do you get if you cross King Kong with shoe polish?

The biggest monkeyshine in the world.

What do you get if you cross the Wolf Man with King Kong?

A very hairy ape.

What do you get if you cross the Wolf Man with a pack of dogs?

A were-woof-woof-woof.

IGOR: Knock-knock.
IVAN: Who's there?
IGOR: Werewolves.
IVAN: Werewolves who?
IGOR: Werewolves are, you won't find me.

KNOCK-KNOCK!

What animated ghost movie was nominated for an Academy Award?

Boo-ty and the Beast.

Why did Mr. and Mrs. Zombie split up?

Their marriage was only "'til death do us part."

What is the one thing a zombie never needs to buy?

Life insurance.

Where do zombies live?

On dead-end streets.

What is a zombie's favorite TV comedy show?

Saturday Night Dead.

Where did the zombie finish in the Transylvania Marathon?

Dead last.

Who is spooky and checks new haunted houses for problems?

The Building Inspectre.

WHAT'S IN A HAUNTED HOUSE?

Alarmed clocks

Frightful decorations

Mon-stairs

Window shudders

Batrooms

Bedglooms

Scream doors

When do ghosts go out haunting?
Whenever the spirit moves them.

What kind of rugs do you find in a haunted house?
No rugs—wail-to-wail carpeting.

WACKY ROBOTS

The Owl Robot—also known as WHO-R-U.
The Cat Robot—also known as KIT-10.
The Rapper Robot—also known as I.M.2-Cool.
The Health Food Robot—also known as GOOD-4-U.

Show me a man who has a metal robot named William . . . and I'll show you a guy with an iron will.

EARTHMAN: Do you recognize the word "Saturn?"
MARTIAN: It has a familiar ring to it.

DAFFYNITION

Astronut: Acorn from space

What aliens like to carve figures out of wood?

The whittle men from Mars.

Why did the alien lawyers go to court?

To settle a space-suit.

MR. SATURN: I'm leaving now.
MS. VENUS: Give me a ring later.

What is the favorite game of monster musicians?

"Maim That Tune."

What is a zombie's favorite rock group?

The Grateful Dead.

How much money does a monster make in a year?

Godzillions.

MAD SCIENTIST: I crossed a witch doctor with a bakery.
GHOUL: What did you get?
MAD SCIENTIST: Voodough.

What happened to the voodoo doll at the restaurant?

It got stuck with the check.

Where does Dracula never go
for dinner?

To a stakehouse.

Why do Egyptian
undertakers make
good detectives?

They're good at
wrapping up their cases.

—— FAMOUS GHOSTS FROM LONG AGO ——

Daniel Boo-ne

Balboo-a

Pocahauntus

Where does a lady ghost sleep?

In her boo-doir.

FRANKENSTEIN: How did you win that varsity
letter?

SASQUATCH: Don't you know I'm a big track star?

Why did the monster try out for the Olympics?

She wanted to win a ghoul medal.

What gum do snakes chew?

Wigley.

How do you make a zombie car?

With a dead battery.

What do haunted chickens lay?

Devilled eggs.

— HOW'S YOUR CREEPY JOB? —

THE INVISIBLE MAN: I can't see myself
working here much longer.

THE WOLF MAN: I'm just moonlighting.

How does a ghostbuster stay in shape?

He rides an exorcise bike.

IGOR: Why is that monster carrying a broom?

IVAN: He's the grim sweeper.

What do you get if you cross an excited owl with an
alien weapon?

A whoo-ray gun.

HA
HA HA
HA HA
HA HA

2

What's gray, weighs five tons, and bounces?

An elephant making
a bungee jump.

What does the sky do when it gets dirty?

It showers.

Which pirate made a lot of mistakes?

Wrong John Silver.

What's brown, lumpy, and goes "choo choo"?

A gravy train.

What did the kiln boss say to the clay pot employee?

"I thought I fired you already."

POLICE CHIEF: Did you follow the crooks across the frozen lake?

COP: Yes, Chief, but they gave me the slip.

SIGN IN A PLANT NURSERY

Final price on trees—take it or leaf it.

AN INSULTING FAREWELL

To a mapmaker: "Get lost!"

To an airline pilot: "Take off!"

To a transferred worker: "Get moving!"

To a *B* Student: "Buzz off!"

To a garbage man: "Haul out of here!"

To a Navy frogman: "Go jump in a lake!"

To an acrobat: "Take a flying leap!"

To a rock musician: "Beat it!"

MACK: How can you keep a nervous horse from running out of the barn?

ZACK: Stall him.

What do you get if you cross a lariat and a magician?

Rope tricks.

JACK: I can make you giggle any time I want to.
MACK: Ha! That's a laugh!

TIME-OUTS

MR. CLOCK: Can I have a minute of your time?
MRS. CLOCK: I'm not tocking to you.

WAITER: What will you have, Mr. Clock?
MR. CLOCK: A minute steak.

PSYCHOLOGIST: You are not a wristwatch.
MRS. CLOCK: I want a second opinion.

What do you say when you bounce
a clock on a trampoline?

"Time's up!"

What did Mrs. Watch say to her
shy son?

"Take your hands off your face."

What did Nanny Wristwatch say to the impatient doorknob?

"Wait your turn. I only have two hands."

What ticks and plays music?

A watchband.

Why did the silly man tattoo alarm clocks on his palms?

He wanted to have time on his hands.

How do sheep keep their feet warm?

They wear wool socks.

How did the sheep get into trouble?

She fell in with a baa-d crowd.

What goes *buzz buzz*, has a hard shell, and gets served on an airplane?

A roasted bee-nut.

What do you get if you cross clothing static with Elvis Presley?

The Kling of Rock and Roll.

What comedian works at the bank?

The joke teller.

What do you call four dirty pigs who sing together?

A barberslop quartet.

What do you get if you cross
bank checks with skunks?

Money odors.

What do you get if you cross
a cold drink with a tent?

An ice teepee.

Why did King Arthur buy
long woolen underwear?

For cold winter knights.

—— THEY'RE A PERFECT MATCH ——

She's cold-hearted . . .

and he lives in Antarctica.

She wears a ponytail . . .

and he likes to horse around.

She's a bad cook . . . and he has no taste.

TED: Why did the Beatles break up?

NED: They started to bug each other.

BEACH BALL: I'm going to
a beach party.

GOLF BALL: Big deal!
I'm going to a tee party.

How do you mail a letter to a fence?

Use the fence post.

TILLIE: A penny for your thoughts?

MILLIE: That makes cents to me.

NUTTY NOTICE

Lumberjacks never die....

They just get the axe.

Where do lumberjacks buy axes?

At a chopping mall.

Why did the margarine buy a rabbit's foot?

It wanted to have butter luck.

FUNNY BUNNIES

What do you get if you cross a banana peel with an accident-prone bunny?

A falling hare.

What organization did Mr. Rabbit join?

The Hare Club for Men.

What do you get if you cross a baby chick with a baby bunny?

Peeper Cottontail.

What should you say when a rabbit sits on an ant hill?

"Look out for bugs, bunny!"

Why was the donkey at the police station?

The cops were trying to pin something on him.

MR. DUCK: Wow! Did you hear the great voice on that young hen?

MR. ROOSTER: Ah, it was just beginner's cluck.

Why was the stork coughing?

He had a frog in his throat.

HA HA HA

HA HA HA

Where do traveling cows mysteriously disappear to?

The Bermooda Triangle.

What do you call a rooster with a bad sunburn?

A fried chicken.

FARMER: My sheep won the million-dollar lottery.

MAN: Lucky ewe!

3

FURNISHED RUMORS

Where should you put a dirty cow?

In a shower stall.

*Show me George
Washington's kitchen . . .
and I'll show you a
presidential cabinet.*

Why did the kitchen
cabinet go to the psychologist?

Because it kept talking to its shelf.

Which piece of furniture plays football?

The end table.

KING ARTHUR: How much do your rooms cost?
INNKEEPER: Twenty dollars per knight.

HUSBAND: I can't decide if we should buy a new bed or not.
WIFE: Me neither. Let's sleep on it.

HOUSE: Ouch! Ouch! Ouch!
CARPENTER: What's wrong with you?
HOUSE: Just window panes.

SIGN FOR A SNOW PLOW COMPANY
Let us break the ice for you.

What do you get if you cross a baseball pitcher with carpeting?

Throw rugs.

What do you get if you cross a foam cushion with an egg?

A padded shell.

HUSBAND: I bought a light bulb that has a four-leaf clover in it.
WIFE: Watt luck!

Which piece of furniture pouts a lot?

The whining room table.

What do you get if you cross a werewolf with a piece of furniture?

A hairy chest.

Why did the dresser turn red?

Its drawers fell down.

What did the dining-room table say at its meeting with the kitchen table?

"Let's find someone to chair our committee."

HA HA HA HA HA HA HA HA HA HA HA HA HA HA HA

How did the TVs celebrate after cable was installed?

They held a great reception.

Why did Mrs. Crow have a big phone bill?

She made too many long-distance caws.

What did the farmer plant in his sofa?

Couch potatoes.

4

LIBRARY LAUGHS

Matt: Did you read *Moby-Dick*?

PAT: Yes, it was a whale of a tale!

MATT: Did you read *Gone with the Wind*?

PAT: Yes, it blew me away.

MATT: How did you like *Dr. Jekyll and Mr. Hyde*?

PAT: It was good and bad.

AL: What is the opposite of a tall tale?
CAL: A short story.

What do comedians read?
Comic books.

What do musicians read?
Notebooks.

What do burglars read?
Crook-books.

What do skunks read?
Best-smellers.

What do cowboys from Dallas read?
Tex-books.

MAN: Do you have any books
on gambling?
LIBRARIAN: You bet!

HA HA HA
HA HA
HA HA

MILLIE: How was that book on chronic illnesses?

TILLIE: Sickening.

LOONY LIBRARY BOOKS

Who Needs a Job? by I. Quitt

Visit Las Vegas by Hy Roller

How to Insult People by U. R. A. Wiseguy

Bathroom Humor by John Potty

How to Make Money by B. A. Counterfeiter

Old Furniture by Ann Teak

Learn to Dance by N. Stepp

Timely Arrivals by Justin Tyme

ED: Do you want this book on how to dig tunnels?

JED: No, it sounds boring.

What kind of vegetables do you always find in the library?

Quiet peas.

What do you get if you cross a library with a golfer?

Book clubs.

What do you get if you cross a library with nocturnal insects?

The Book of the Moth Club.

What do you need to be a good librarian?

Shelf-control.

What did the librarian say when the duck rustled his feathers noisily?

"Quiet down!"

HAIRDRESSER: What kind of hairstyle would you like?

LIBRARIAN: A pageboy.

CARPENTER: I need a title that shows how to build a bookcase.

LIBRARIAN: Try the shelf-help section.

WOMAN: Did Farmer Green come into the library today?

LIBRARIAN: Yes. He's in our weeding room.

Knock-knock!

Who's there?

Rhoda.

Rhoda who?

Rhoda novel, but no one will read it.

WRITER: Just call me Ball Point.

EDITOR: Why?

WRITER: It's my pen name.

PRIEST: I'm looking for good books about Catholic sisters.

LIBRARIAN: Try our nun-fiction section.

EDITOR: The King of England just wrote a book.

PUBLISHER: I guess he expects royalties.

What should you give a book when it's cold?

A book cover.

5

ALPHA-BITS

What did the alphabet say after it fell down?

I-M-O-K.

Which channel do letters of the alphabet watch?

MTV.

Where does Mr. Alphabet sit when he comes home from work?

In his EZ chair.

What does the alphabet wear on warm days?

A T-shirt.

What monsters do you find in the haunted alphabet?

Killer Bs.

Which letters make a great couple?

U-N-ME.

Which letters and number make a great cheer?

I-M-4-U!

Which letters and number can never go on a diet?

I-8-IT-ALL.

Which letters and number can tell you to be careful?

B-4-WARNED!

What kind of sale did the number store have?

2-4-1.

Which number and letters always get into trouble?

2-BAD.

Which letters in the alphabet are the smartest?

I-M.

MACK: What did the tired man say to the alphabet?

ZACK: Can I catch some Zs?

Which two letters mean you look nice?

Q-T.

Which letter of the alphabet do you find on roads and highways?

The U-turn.

Which letter of the alphabet is never late?

B-on-time.

Which letter of the alphabet do you find near the ocean?

The Cport.

HA HA
HA HA
HA HA HA
HA HA

What kind of soup does the alphabet like best?

P soup.

Which letter and number when put together
mean victory?

I-1.

What do you get
if you cross a letter
of the alphabet with
a green vegetable?

T-peas.

6

FUN FOOD

Why did the ghost go into the kitchen?
To scare up some food.

What did the termites
have for dinner?
Table scraps.

What does a hungry garbage truck eat?
Junk food.

What do you get if you cross gossip with soft margarine?
Rumors you can spread easily.

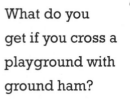

What do you get if you cross a playground with ground ham?

Park sausage.

Why did the witch go into the kitchen?

To brew some coffee.

What monster makes loud noises while drinking soda?

The sea slurpent.

What food is made out of young reptiles that practice the martial arts?

Teenage mutant ninja turtle soup.

How do you make a werewolf breathe fire?

Feed him chili puppers.

DAFFYNITION

Vegetarians: people you don't have to meat

FUN FOOD BOOKS

How to Prepare Meals by I. Ken Cook

Tasty Recipes by Etta Belle Food

Better Breakfasts by Ronny Eggs

Fish for Supper by Sam N. Stake

1,001 Sandwich Recipes by Cole Supper

What did the beaver eat at the restaurant?

A tree-course meal.

What vegetable do Alaskan sled dogs like?

Mushed potatoes.

Knock-knock.

Who's there?

Rice.

Rice who?

Rice and shine.

CUSTOMER: I'd like a tasty dish.

WAITER: You're supposed to eat our food, sir, not our dishes.

Hotdog packagers—
we're not losers . . . we're wieners!

Why did the foxes move next door to a rabbit family?

So they could have their neighbors over for dinner.

Why should you never invite a clock to dinner?

They always have seconds.

WAITER: Would you like to have a menu?
CUSTOMER: No, I'd rather have some food, please.

What did the lovesick lettuce say to the stove?

"You're baking my heart."

What did the head of lettuce take to school?

A loose-leaf binder.

NUTTY NOTICE

Jack Frost likes cold cuts.

WACKY WANT AD

Cook needed for restaurant—
must wok for a living.

CEREAL: What do you want to do tonight?
MILK: Let's go bowling.

What did the scientist get when he crossed a
mattress with an oven?

Breakfast in bed.

What diet guru lives in Transylvania?

Count Calories.

Which Beatles song was about a deli treat?

"Yellow Submarine Sandwich."

Knock-knock!

Who's there?

Frosting.

Frosting who?

Frosting in the morning, brush your teeth.

ED: Do bananas wear shoes?

FRED: No, they always wear slippers.

What do you get if you cross cooking fat with coconut trees?

Greased palms.

COOK: How can I think up new recipes for pasta?

WAITER: Use your noodle.

Why wouldn't the little watch's mother serve him dinner?

Because he didn't wash his hands.

What do you get if you cross dinner with a watch?

Mealtime.

Corn farmers—let us box your ears.

Knock-knock!
   Who's there?
Venice.
   Venice who?
Venice lunch? I'm starved.

Knock-knock!
   Who's there?
Wilma.
   Wilma who?
Wilma dinner be ready soon?

Knock-knock!
   Who's there?
Barbie.
   Barbie who?
Barbie-Q my steak.

KNOCK-KNOCK!

What do sharks eat at barbecues?
   Clamburgers.

43

7

JUST KIDDING

Who tells nursery rhymes and is lumpy?

Mother Goosebumps.

Who lives in Mother Goose Land and is made of cabbage?

Old King Coleslaw.

What monster lives in Mother Goose Land?

Little Bo Creep.

Why did Simple Simon take a trunk to the doctor's office?

He had a chest cold.

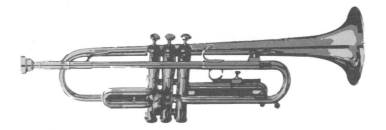

When does the trumpet player blow his horn?

When he drives his car.

NUTTY NOTICE

Humpty Dumpty is a great guy, but
he has scrambled eggs for brains!

MOTHER: Why did you spend all your allowance
on candy?

BOY: Dad said to put my money where my mouth is.

CHIEF: What cable music channel did you get in
your tent?

MEDICINE MAN: MTP.

BOY: I flunked all of my courses. I flunked all of my
courses.

MOM: Why did you say that twice?

BOY: Teacher told me I have to repeat this grade.

Why did the wristwatch get an A on the math test?

He knew his times tables.

BOY: Dad, I want to be a comedian.
FATHER: Don't make me laugh.

MATT: What do I get if I become an apprentice knight?
SIR MORGAN: Three squire meals a day.

What did the boy say when he saw a buzzing insect land on a clock?

Bee on time.

BOY: I can't believe I have all this math homework.
GIRL: Don't bother me. I have problems of my own.

Why did the silly math student go to the bakery?

To find pi.

SIGN ON A PLAYGROUND EQUIPMENT COMPANY
Come to Our Slide Show.

Why did the squirrel gnaw through the side of the house?

He was looking for wallnuts.

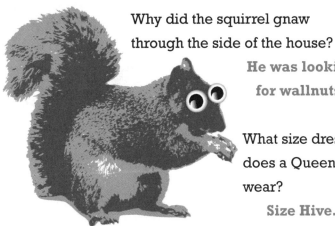

What size dress does a Queen Bee wear?

Size Hive.

What do you get if you cross cows with party games?

Moosical chairs.

What musical toy is the most athletic?

The jock-in-the-box.

HA HA HA HA HA HA HA HA HA HA HA HA HA HA HA HA HA HA HA HA HA HA HA HA HA HA HA

SNOOPY: Did you see that new cartoon strip?

BROWNIE: No, I covered my eyes.

What does Tinkerbell drink from?

A pixie cup.

ED: What did the policeman say to the playground equipment?

NED: "You can't park here."

LINNY: Did you buy duck feathers?

GINNY: Yes. They were marked down.

What do you get if you cross a jogger with a four-leaf clover?

A run of good luck.

What chorus line performs at the prehistoric Radio City Music Hall?

The Bedrock-ettes.

CRAZY CHRISTMAS GREETINGS

From a frog: Have a hoppy holiday season.

From the Internal Revenue Service:

Many happy returns.

From a honey maker: Bee happy.

From a spice merchant:

Seasoning's greetings.

From a cereal maker: Crispness greetings.

From a grower of Christmas plants:

Happy holly-days.

From a vegetable farmer: Peas on earth.

Why did Santa Clause wear a cowboy hat and cowboy boots?

He was going to a western ho-ho-hoedown.

What do you get if you cross Santa Claus with a flying saucer?

A U-F-HO HO HO!

Why didn't Scrooge mind getting coal for Christmas?

It helped him cut down on his heating bill.

What goes, "Baa, baa, baa humbug!"?

Ebeneezer Sheep.

What is Santa's favorite cowboy song?

"Ho-Ho-Home on the Range."

Who brings presents to skunks on Christmas?

Scent Nicholas.

What did Santa do at the barber shop?

Trimmed the Christmas trees.

8

KNOCK-KNOCK!

Knock-knock!
Who's there?
Omen.
Omen who?
Omen a bad mood!

Knock-knock!
Who's there?
Celery.
Celery who?
Celery dance?

Knock-knock!
    Who's there?
Distress.
    Distress who?
Distress matches my shoes.

Knock-knock!
    Who's there?
Eileen.
    Eileen who?
Eileen over to
tie my shoes.

Knock-knock!
    Who's there?
Esau.
    Esau who?
Esau you coming
and left.

Knock-knock!
    Who's there?
Gwen.
    Gwen who?
Gwen you leave, close
the door.

Knock-knock!
    Who's there?
Habit.
    Habit who?
Habit your way.

Knock-knock!
    Who's there?
Hairs.
    Hairs who?
Hairs another fine
mess you've gotten
me into.

Knock-knock!
   Who's there?
Irish.
   Irish who?
Irish I knew. I have amnesia.

Knock-knock!
   Who's there?
I, Toad.
   I, Toad who?
I Toad you I was coming over!

Knock-knock!
   Who's there?
Jamaica.
   Jamaica who?
Jamaica my lunch yet?

Knock-knock!
   Who's there?
Kennel.
   Kennel who?
Kennel come out if you ask him nicely.

Knock-knock!
   Who's there?
Kenya.
   Kenya who?
Kenya come on out and play?

KNOCK-KNOCK!

Knock-knock!
   Who's there?
Less.
   Less who?
Less go shopping!

Knock-knock!
   Who's there?
Luke.
   Luke who?
Luke out for
falling rocks.

Knock-knock!
   Who's there?
Menace.
   Menace who?
Menace the plural
of *man*.

Knock-knock!
   Who's there?
Mist.
   Mist who?
You mist me!

Knock-knock!
   Who's there?
Rapper.
   Rapper who?
Rapper in a blanket.
She's cold.

Knock-knock!
    Who's there?
Recited.
    Recited who?
Recited the enemy,
and we fired.

Knock-knock!
    Who's there?
Reveal.
    Reveal who?
Reveal sorry for you.

Knock-knock!
    Who's there?
Tillie.
    Tillie who?
Tillie apologizes,
I won't forgive him.

Knock-knock!
    Who's there?
Retail.
    Retail who?
Retail stories around
the campfire.

Knock-knock!
    Who's there?
Sandy.
    Sandy who?
Sandy dirty clothes
to the cleaners.

Knock-knock!
    Who's there?
Three chairs.
    Three chairs
    who?
Three chairs for the
home team!

Knock-knock!
Who's there?
Urn.
Urn who?
Urn your keep.

Knock-knock!
Who's there?
Vera.
Vera who?
Vera you hiding?

Knock-knock!
Who's there?
I, Wanda.
I, Wanda who?
I Wanda where I put the house key?

Knock-knock!
Who's there?
Wheat.
Wheat who?
Wheat just a moment, please.

Knock-knock!
Who's there?
Wilder.
Wilder who?
Wilder out, let's raid the refrigerator.

Knock-knock!
Who's there?
Willie.
Willie who?
Willie show up on time?

Knock-knock!
    Who's there?
Wren.
    Wren who?
Wren in Rome, do
as the Romans do!

Knock-knock!
    Who's there?
Yaw.
    Yaw who?
Way to cheer,
cowboy!

Knock-knock!
    Who's there?
Yawl.
    Yawl who?
Yawl be sorry.

Knock-knock!
    Who's there?
Yukon.
    Yukon who?
Yukon open the
door—it's safe.

9

VETS, PETS, AND SOMETHING WET

Pet-shop owner: You can't return that chimp.

MAN: Why not? Don't you have a monkey-back guarantee?

What do sloppy cats leave behind after a picnic?

Kitty litter.

ZACK: The hero of this jungle book is a lion.

MACK: How do you know that?

ZACK: He's the mane character.

VET: Where do you keep your sled dogs?

ALASKAN GUIDE: In a mush room.

What do you get if you cross an oak with a Saint Bernard?

A tree with very loud bark.

Why did the dog go to court?

To pay a barking ticket.

VET: Your dog's nose isn't too hot.

BOY: His ears are ugly, too, but I love him anyway.

Which Egyptian dog ruler died very young?

King Mutt.

What do you get if you cross Lassie with a rose bush?

Collie-flowers.

What did the telephone operator say to the dog?

"You have a bone call."

What did the teacher say to the pig farmers?

"Don't talk unless you raise your hams."

JOCKEY: Doc, is my sick horse all right?
VET: Yes, he's in stable condition.

What's wooly and floats in the ocean?

A cruise sheep.

What do you say when a sheep sneezes?

"Bless ewe!"

Which sea creature is very sloppy?

The Loch Mess Monster.

ZACK: Which kind of fish swim alone?
MACK: Ones that haven't had any schooling.

What does a medieval farmer use to ride the waves?

A serf board.

What do sharks eat for dessert?

Fish cakes.

How do you catch an elephant fish?

Bait your hook with a peanut.

What has a rod, reel, and mane?

A fishing lion.

What kind of pet would you find in a jewelry store?

A goldfish.

ED: What kind of vehicle does Sergeant Goldfish drive?

JED: A fish tank.

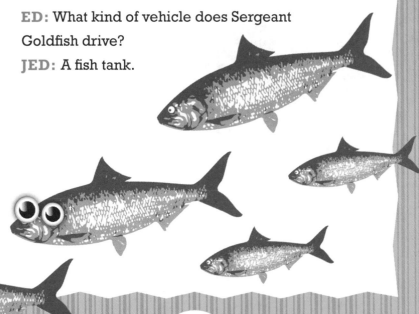

What do squids ride to school on?
    An octobus.

What famous explorer swims underwater a lot?
    Jockes Cousteau.

What gymnastic stunt do fish like to perform?
    Carp-wheels.

What do you get if you cross an octopus and a shark?
    An animal armed to the teeth.

HA HA HA

What's soaking wet and wears a suit of armor?

A rainy knight.

What do you call a seasick ogre?

A green giant.

What did the vet say to the anxious buzzing insect?

"Bee patient."

HA HA HA HA HA HA HA HA HA HA HA HA HA HA HA HA HA HA HA HA

10

THAT'S WHEELIE FUNNY!

What do you get if you cross a comedian with a bicycle?

Someone who is wheel funny.

What do you get if you cross turtles with automobiles?

Very slow traffic!

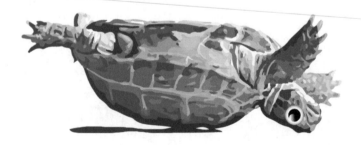

What do you find in a dinosaur junkyard?

T. Wrecks.

What has four wheels and goes "*Urp! Urp! Urp!*"?

A hiccup truck.

What do pigs use to carry their groceries?

Slopping carts.

Where does a car engine live?

In a motor home.

What's covered with red spots and drives cars into brick walls?

A rash dummy.

Why didn't the silly kid graduate from driving school?

She couldn't pass.

What has feathers and operates an 18-wheeler?

A cluck driver.

What kind of shoes with wheels do penguins wear?

Polar-skates.

What does Mother Air Rifle use to take her infant for a walk?

A BB carriage.

SALESMAN: Would you like to buy a car battery?
CUSTOMER: Only if you'll charge it.

What is the automobile's favorite TV game show?

Wheel of Fortune.

What has wheels and goes *slosh, slosh*?

A carpool.

What kind of car did the elephant want?

One with lots of trunk space.

What do you get if you cross an automobile with a pot of glue?

A car with a sticky shift.

What happens when boy tire meets a girl tire?

They go around together.

What was the miniature automobile model made of?

Car-d stock.

What kind of transportation do ballerinas take?

Tutu trains.

LOCOMOTIVE TO A BOXCAR:
Watch it pal, I've got a lot of
pull around here.

Why did the locomotive
feel so important?

It was a track star.

CONDUCTOR: Why are you insulting that old
locomotive?
ENGINEER: Because it works best when it's all
steamed up.

What locomotives do you see in fashion magazines?

Model trains.

SILLY SLOGANS

Road Map Publishers—
we know where we're going.
Steering Wheel Company—
let us turn things around for you.
Bird Candy Makers—a sweet tweet for your pet!

What has lots of wheels and looks like a big bee?

A Greyhound buzz.

How do you drive a cattle car?

Steer it.

What has a mirror and four wheels?

A compact car.

What honks a lot and has wheels?

A flock of geese on a bus.

What has two wheels and laughs a lot?

A ha-ha-Harley Davidson motorcycle.

What insect has four wheels and lives at the beach?

The dune buggy.

CAR: Why is that baby tire crying?
AUTO: It needs to be changed.

Why couldn't the tire buy anything?
It was flat broke.

What do you put on toasted cars?
Traffic jam.

Why did the sheep driver tie up traffic?
He kept making ewe turns.

ZACK: That car has claws on its hood.
MACK: It's probably a taxicrab.

Why did the car have an upset stomach?
It had too much gas.

What famous car lives in a church tower?
The Hatchback of Notre Dame.

How did the car pass its demolition derby test?
It took a crash course.

ZACK: That locomotive isn't too smart.
MACK: That's because it has a one-track mind.

Where do big trucks go to have fun?

To a trailer park.

What do you call an antelope that sells cars?

A gnu car dealer.

What do you get if you cross an automobile with a kangaroo?

A car that's easy to jump-start.

What does a car need to be a great athlete?

Good motor skills.

Where should you take a damaged car?

To a bruised car lot.

What has four wheels, pulls cars, and goes "Ouch!"?

A sore toe truck.

Knock-knock!

Who's there?

Wheel.

Wheel who?

Wheel see you later.

KNOCK-KNOCK!

Why did the stupid driver let his car crash?

He didn't want to brake it.

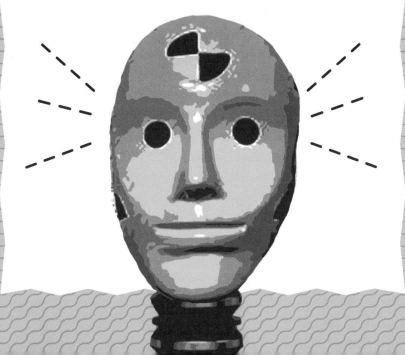

Why did the new car talk so much?

> It came equipped with a hot-air bag.

What do tires wear to keep warm?

> Hub caps.

Why did the police cars go to the automobile junkyard?

> To look for car hoodlums.

What should you do with a wet tire?

> Spin-dry it.

AL: How did you know your car was in pain?
HAL: Its brakes kept screeching.

What did the car say to the gas pump?

> "You can't fuel me!"

What do you get if you cross an executioner and a plane with no motor?

> A hang glider.

What do you get if you cross a jet and a motorcycle?

> A sonic *vroom*.

What holds eight passengers and is totally out of sight?

The Invisible Van.

Show me a motorist who has a fender bender with a police car ... and I'll show you a driver who's had a run-in with the law.

MAN: How much do these old batteries cost?
CLERK: Nothing. They're free of charge.

What does Minnie Mouse drive?

A Minnievan.

11

Why did the sorceress go to beauty school?

To learn to wave her wand.

MARY: I make pressed flowers for a living.
LARRY: Is it fun?
MARY: No. It's cut and dry.

EMPLOYEE: Boss, my mind is shot.
BOSS: Oh, yeah? Well,
I do the firing around here.

What do you get if you cross a thundercloud with a checkbook?

Rain checks.

What do you get if you cross a checkbook with a math teacher?

Money problems.

What do you get if you cross a gardener and a fortune teller?

Someone who weeds palms.

ZACK: How's your exterminator business?
MACK: I'm still working out the bugs.

TED: Do you like being a watch repairman?
ED: It has its moments.

SON: I want to be a minister.
DAD: Heaven help you!

NUTTY NOTICE
Playwrights put words
in other people's mouths.

THE DIZZY DOCTOR

"Doctor, doctor, my wife thinks she's an acrobat."
"I'll stop her from flipping out."

"Doctor, doctor, my husband thinks he's a car."
"Don't let him drive you crazy."

"Doctor, doctor, my daughter thinks
she's a sheet of music."
"Bring her in, and I'll take some notes."

"Doctor, doctor, I keep thinking about
rubber bands."
"Well, snap out of it!"

"Doctor, doctor, you've got to help
me. I think I'm a kangaroo."
"Quick, hop up on my couch!"

"Doctor, doctor, I'm sick as
a dog!"
**"I know a good vet I can
send you to."**

BONE DOCTOR:
Business is really bad.
NURSE: What you need is
a lucky break.

Why did the math teacher
go to a psychologist?
> He needed help with
> his problems.

What do you call a person who pushes a broom
and snores?
> A sweepwalker.

What marshal works for the Internal Revenue
Service?
> A Taxes ranger.

LAW STUDENT #1: Let's pretend we're in court.
LAW STUDENT #2: I'm not in the moot.

EDITOR: Why do you print your books on
flypaper?
PUBLISHER: So people can't put them down.

What do lady roller skaters wear to fancy parties?
High-wheeled shoes.

*Show me a math teacher who becomes a minister . . .
and I'll show you a guy who counts his blessings.*

*Show me a king with a sore throat . . . and I'll show
you a guy with a royal pain in the neck.*

MR. SMITH: Why aren't you president of the
mortgage company anymore?
MR. JONES: Frankly, I lost interest.

WACKY WANT AD
Camera shop needs dark room assistant—
work with us and see what develops.

CRAZY COMPANY SLOGANS

Wooden Doors: Go ahead! Knock our product.

Lawn Service School: We'll show you how to make mow money.

Jump-Rope School: Skip class.

Leather Company: We have lots to hide.

Speedy Communications: Let us give you the fax.

Video Game Company: We're in business for the fun of it.

The V Motor Company: We're right behind U.

ANDY: What does a witch teacher use to correct spelling tests?

RANDY: A magic marker.

What does a Transylvanian dentist use to pull out fangs?

Vampliers.

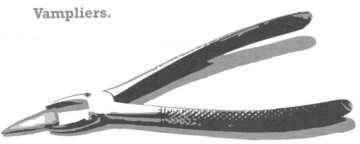

SIGNING OFF

Sign on a window shade company:

Love is not always blinds.

Sign in an air-conditioned banquet hall:

We'll always give you a cool reception.

Sign on a music school:

Students are allowed to play during class.

Sign in a shoelace-testing plant:

Knot during working hours.

How do you fire a lady who works in an underwear department?

Give her a pink slip.

NUTTY NOTICE

Never date barbers.

They give everyone the brush-off.

What did the policeman say to the lumberjack?

"Chop in the name of the law."

SILLY SLOGANS

Baseball Umpires' Union:
We decide when to call strikes.

Basketball Refs' Union: Experts in foul play.

Fence Installers' Union: We have great picket lines.

Housekeepers' Union: Don't mess with us.

Bakers' Union: Bake us an offer.

Airplane Pilots' Union: We demand high pay.

WHAT KIND OF MUSIC DO YOU LIKE?

"Heavy metal," said the iron worker.

"Hard rock," said the geologist.

"Bluegrass," said the gardener.

"Swing," said the playground equipment
manufacturer.

"Pop music," said the father-to-be.

Why did the coach send a monster into the
football game?

Because his team needed a field ghoul.

HA HA HA HA HA HA HA HA HA

HOW'S BUSINESS?

Toupee company: Business has been falling off.

Steak company: Things are tough.

Clock company: Times are bad.

Furnace company: We're in hot water.

Show me a man who's putting a roof over a clock tower . . . and I'll show you a man who's working overtime.

What does King Kong use to fix a leaky pipe?

A monkey wrench.

What football player drinks a lot of lemon juice?

The bitter end.

12

CHUCKLE CHILLERS

What's scary and carries swords?

The Three Boo-sketeers.

What do you do if you get if you cross Dr. Jekyll with a playground?

Dr. Jekyll and
Mr. Slide.

What game does Dr. Jekyll love to play?

Hyde-and-go-seek.

SANDI: I'm in love with the Invisible Man.

MANDI: What do you see in him?

MAD SCIENTIST: I crossed a witch doctor with morning mist.

GHOUL: What did you get?

MAD SCIENTIST: Voodew.

What did everyone say when the witch walked down the aisle?

"Here comes the bride and broom."

What does a witch wear on her wrist?

A charm bracelet.

What did the witch say after she buried her treasure?

"Hex marks the spot!"

Why did the witch go to the hospital?

She needed some hex-rays.

What do witches sell at flea markets?

Witchcrafts.

HA HA HA

CREEP: Does Dracula play tennis?

GHOUL: No, but he loves bat-minton.

How did Dracula break his fangs?

Learning you can't get blood from a stone.

✂ -

WACKY WANT AD

Dracula wants to meet a girl

with an appetite for adventure.

Object: To go out for a bite.

Why did Dracula climb up on the barn roof?

To get to the weather vein.

Why would Dracula make a good policeman?

He'd take a bite out of crime.

Why did Dracula run away from the gold rush?

A prospector wanted to stake a claim.

What does Dracula use to make
vampire pancakes?

Bat-ter.

Knock-knock!

Who's there?

Eben.

Eben who?

Eben bitten by
a vampire.

Which dinosaur is Dracula
afraid of?

The Stakeasaurus.

DRACULA: I just bit a dwarf on the neck.
VAMPIRE: Oh, Drac! How could you stoop so low!

ZACK: Does Dr. Frankenstein like to do aerobics?
MACK: Nah, he's a body builder.

What do you call a cowboy who jumps on
Frankenstein's monster's back and yells
"Giddyup!"?

A cowpoke who rides the strange.

— WHY DID FRANKENSTEIN'S MONSTER — GO TO A PSYCHIATRIST?

. . . He thought he had a screw loose.

. . . He felt like he was coming apart at the seams.

. . . He couldn't pull himself together.

What is Dr. Frankenstein's favorite therapy?

Shock treatments.

IVAN: Dracula refused to run a race against Frankenstein's monster.

IGOR: Why?

IVAN: Because he thought the competition was too stiff.

MRS. WOLF: There's a ghoul in your kitchen.

MRS. FRANKENSTEIN: Relax. That's just our housecreeper.

What has fangs and flies?

A werewolf on a hang glider.

Why did the werewolf hold his hand up to his ear?

Because he always listened to his paw.

ZACK: Why did the mad doctor go to the cemetery?

MACK: To treat a grave illness.

What did the mad doctor say to Igor while he was building his monster?

"Hey, come here and give me a hand."

Which famous ape writes best-selling horror novels?

Stephen King Kong.

What do you call an author who keeps turning out books after he dies?

A ghostwriter.

What monsters live in a nice house in the Italian countryside?

Godvilla.

NAT: Godzilla's in New York!

PAT: I guess he's polishing off the Big Apple.

What giant monster has a pea brain?

Podzilla.

Which giant monster is really clumsy?

Clutzilla.

What city devoured by Godzilla refused to stay down?

Tokyo-yo.

WACKY WANT AD

Godzilla wants to meet a giant lady monster.

Object: To step out on the town.

What do you get if you cross Godzilla with Merlin's magic wand?

A lizard wizard.

What does Godzilla have on the walls of his bathroom?

Rep-tiles.

IGOR: Why did the children of the corn get lost?

IVAN: They couldn't find their way out of the maize.

Knock-knock!

> Who's there?

Eerie.

> Eerie who?

Eerie is! Grab him before he escapes!

Knock-knock!

> Who's there?

I, Spectre.

> I, Spectre, who?

I Spectre to scream any minute!

What monster goes "Caw! Caw!" and lives in the Himalayan Mountains?

> The Abominable Crowman.

What does the Abominable Snowman put his ice cream in?

> A snow-cone.

Where did Cinderella Yeti go?

　　To the snow ball.

Knock-knock!

　　Who's there?

Icy.

　　Icy who?

Icy you, but you can't see me.

KNOCK-KNOCK!

What do you get if you cross a yeti with a turtle?

　　The Abominable Slowman.

What does the Abominable Snowman have for breakfast?

　　Frosted Flakes.

What does the Abominable Snowman eat at a ballgame?

　　A chilly dog.

What does the Abominable Snowman eat on Thanksgiving Day?

　　Cold turkey.

What does the Abominable Snowman
eat for dessert?

Frozen custard.

What does the health-conscious
Abominable Snowman eat at snack time?

Frozen yogurt.

What does the Abominable Snowman use in
his coffee?

Cold creamer.

NUTTY NOTICE

The mummy loves wrap music!

SNOWMAN'S SHOPPING LIST

Cold cuts

Iced tea

Popsicles

Frozen dinners

BIZARRE BOOKS

- - - - - - - - - - - - - - - -

My Life as a Werewolf
by Harry Beast

I Don't Want to Be a Zombie
by Barry McQuick

The Homeless Vampire
by Anita Coffin

Godzilla's Cookbook
by I. Etta City

The Invisible Man Disappears
by I. M. Gone

My House Is Haunted
by I. Shaw Ghosts

WEIRD WORDS OF WISDOM

On the tomb of a memory expert:

"Gone but not forgotten"

On the tomb of a custodian:

"Sweep in peace"

On the tomb of a comedian:

"Jest in peace"

On the tomb of a housekeeper:

"Duster to dust!"

On the tomb of a short-order cook:

"Hashes to ashes"

Show me Bigfoot running a marathon . . . and I'll show you some of the world's biggest race tracks!

Why did Mr. Skeleton wear a hat on the middle of his leg?

It was a knee cap.

NUTTY NOTICE
The Abominable Snowman drinks
freeze-dried coffee.

What do police ghosts wear under their coats?

Boo-letproof vests.

What's ugly, wears feathers, and dances in a chorus line in Las Vegas?

Show ghouls.

Which two letters of the alphabet say good-bye?

C-U.

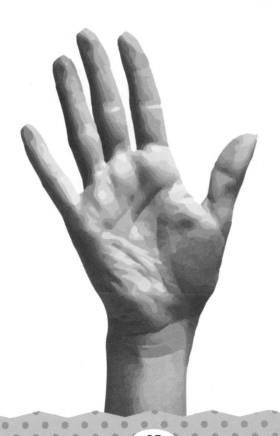